POP PIANO HITS

SIMPLE ARRANGEMENTS FOR STUDENTS OF ALL AGES

# Roar, Royals & More Hot Singles

ISBN 978-1-4803-6655-8

HAL•LEONARD®
CORPORATION

7777 W. BLUEMOUND RD. P.O. BOX 13819 MILWAUKEE, WI 53213

Visit Hal Leonard Online at
**www.halleonard.com**

# Contents

# ATLAS
## from THE HUNGER GAMES: CATCHING FIRE

Words and Music by GUY BERRYMAN,
JON BUCKLAND, WILL CHAMPION
and CHRIS MARTIN

Some saw the sun,

some saw the smoke,
Some far a - way,

some heard the gun,
some search for gold,

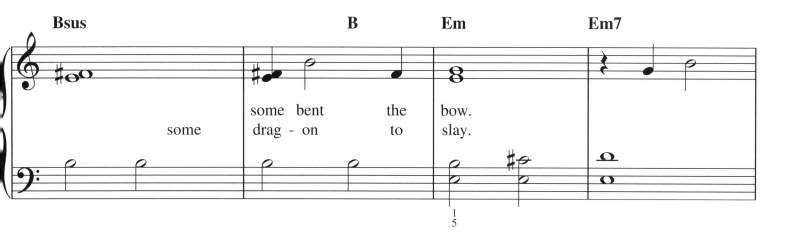

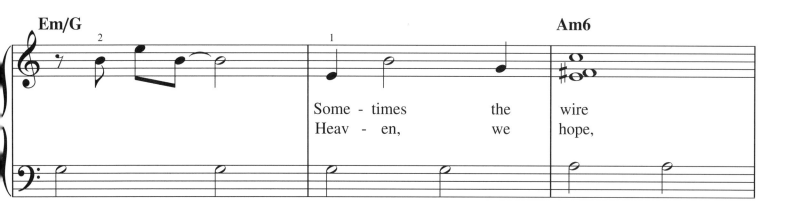

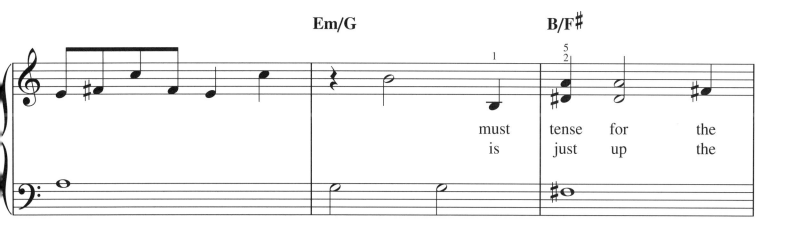

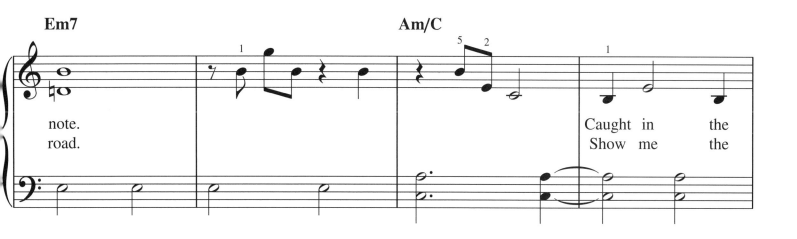

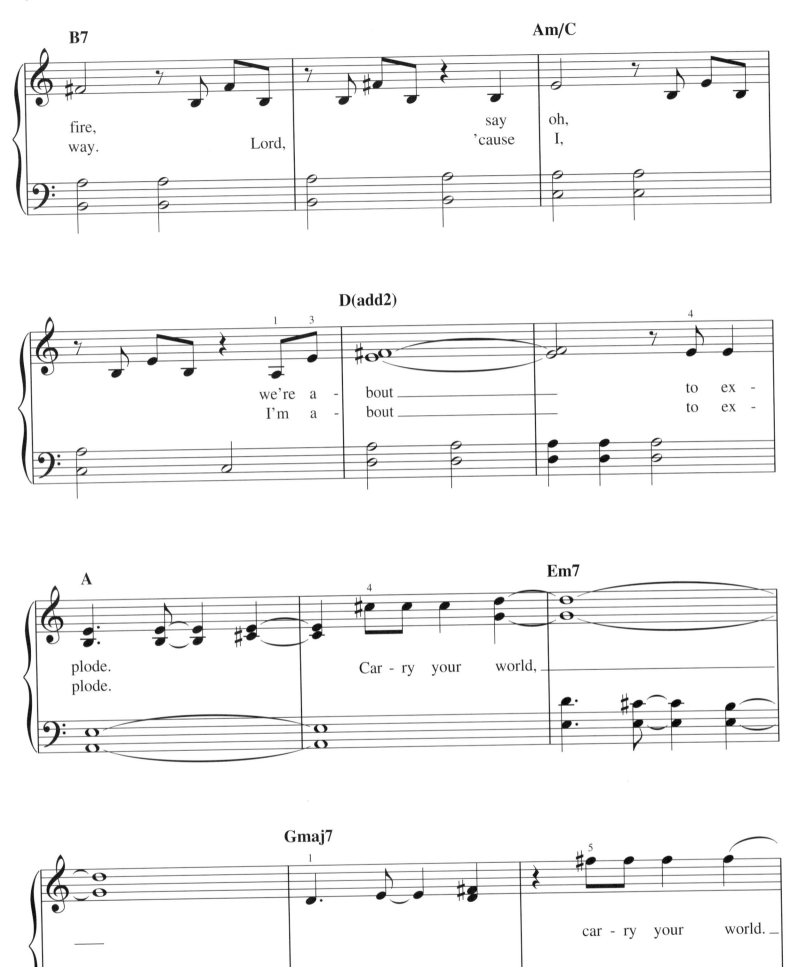

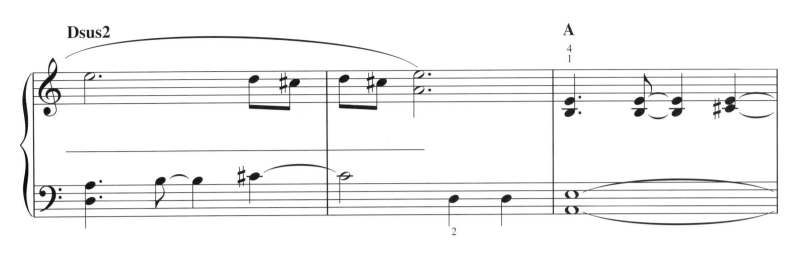

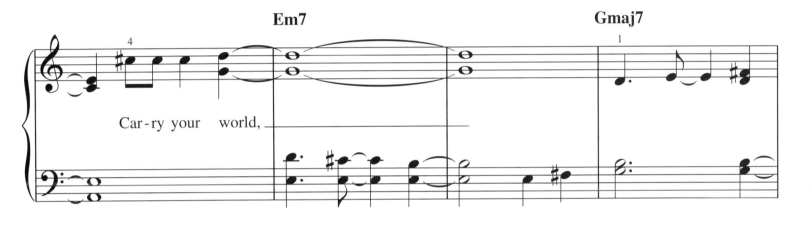

Car-ry your world,

car-ry your world.

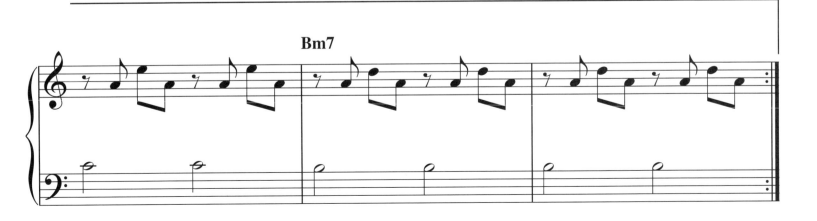

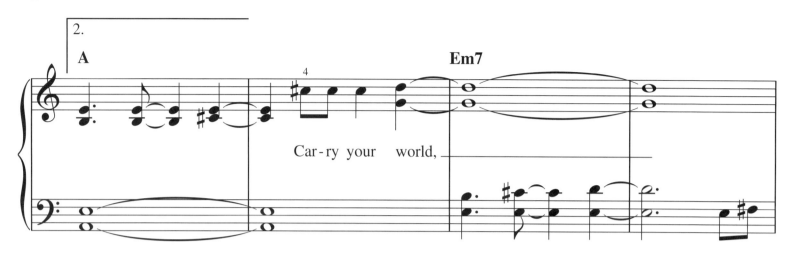

2.

A

Em7

Car - ry your world,

Gmaj7

Dsus

and all your hurt.

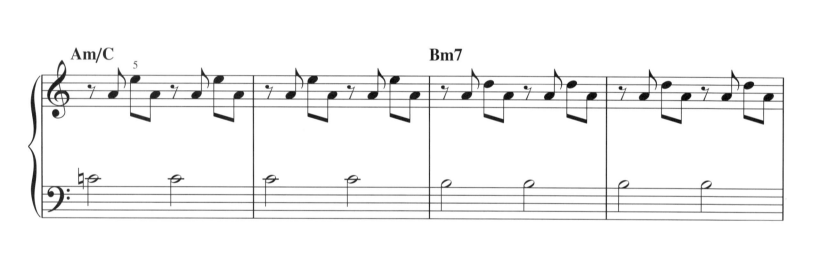

Am/C

Bm7

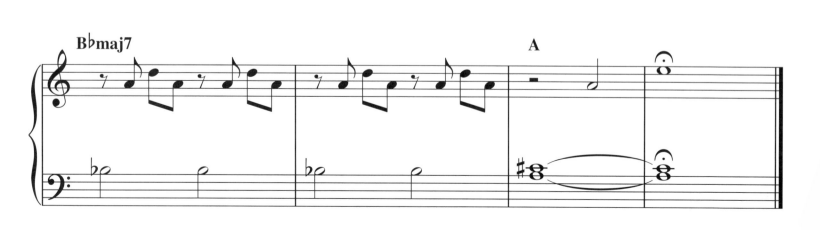

B♭maj7

A

# ROAR

Words and Music by KATY PERRY,
BONNIE McKEE, MAX MARTIN,
LUKASZ GOTTWALD and HENRY WALTER

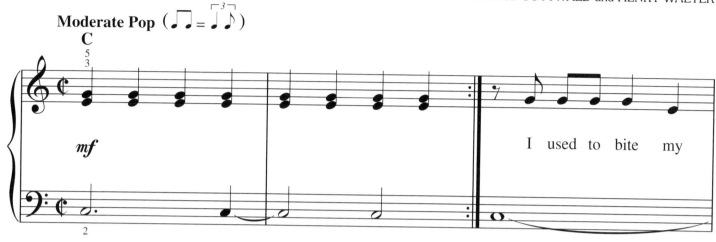

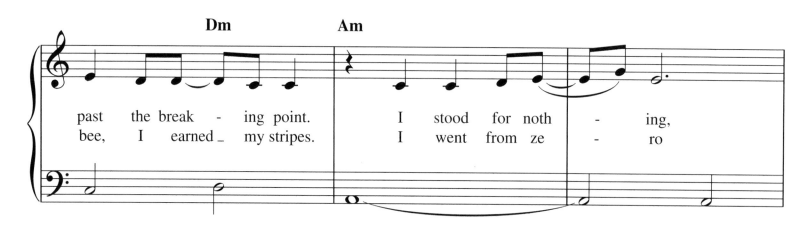

hear my voice, you hear that sound ___ like thun - der gon - na

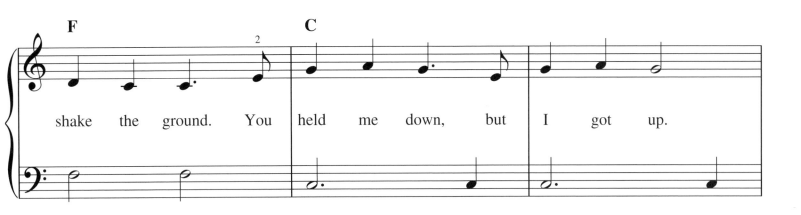

shake the ground. You held me down, but I got up.

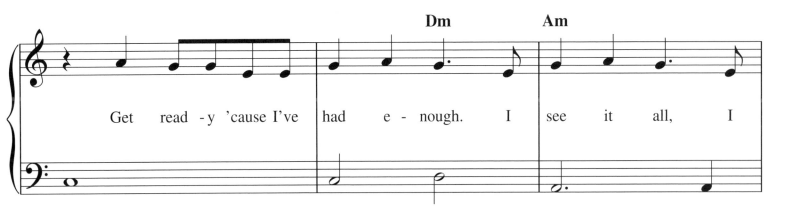

Get read - y 'cause I've had e - nough. I see it all, I

see it now. I got the eye of the ti -

12

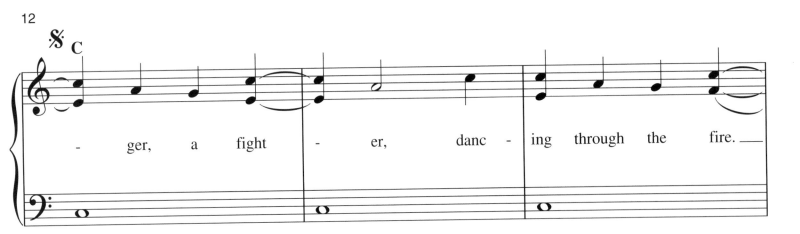

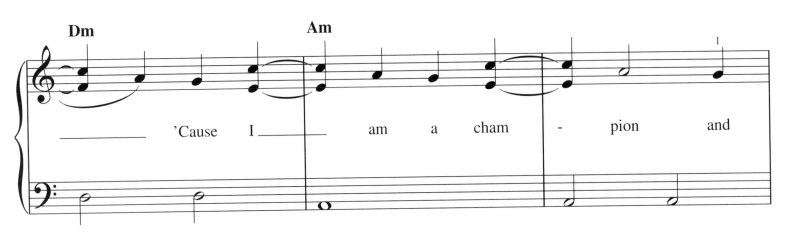

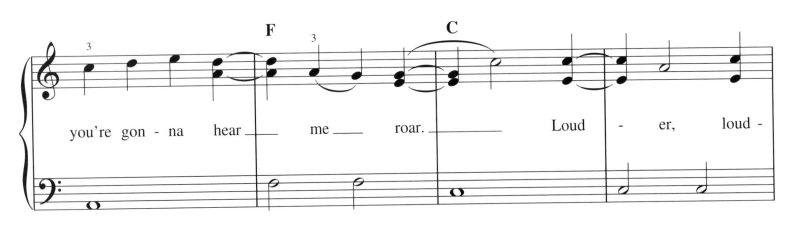

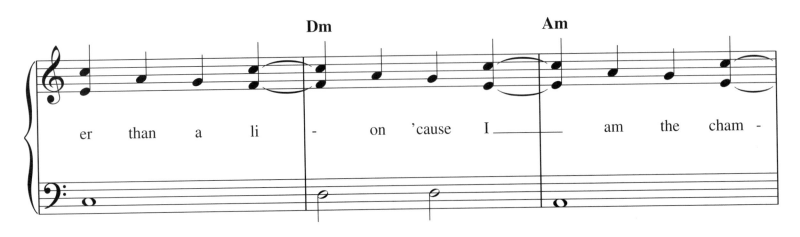

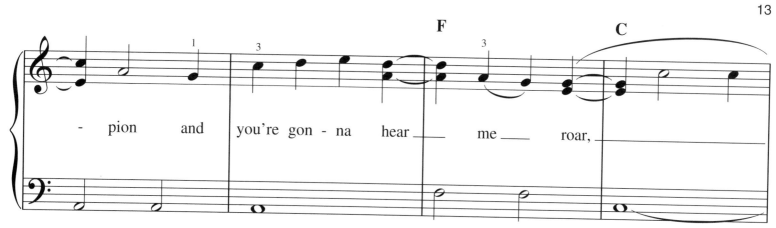

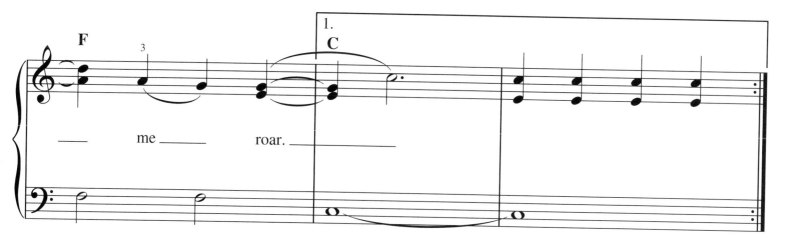

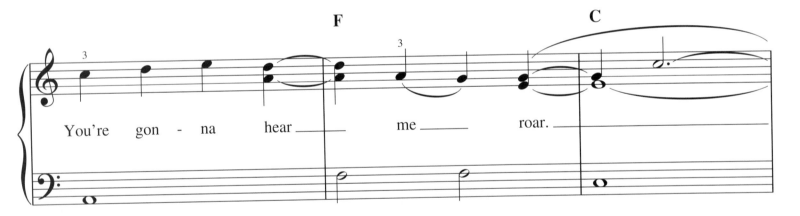

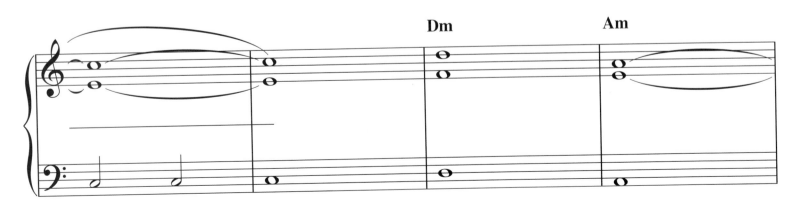

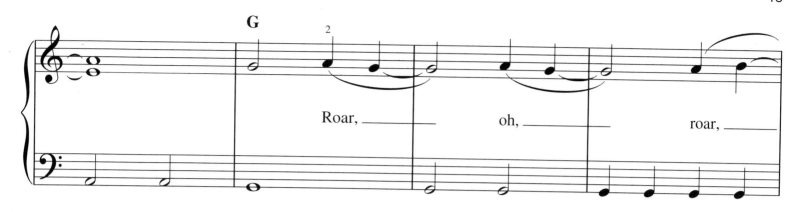

Roar, _____ oh, _____ roar, _____

_____ oh, _____ roar. _____

**D.S. al Coda**
**(take 2nd ending)**

**CODA**

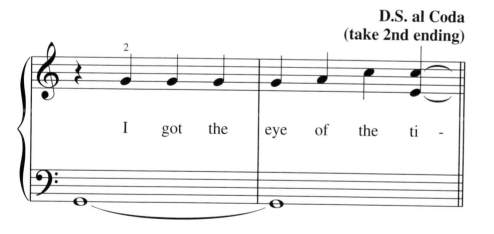

I got the eye of the ti -

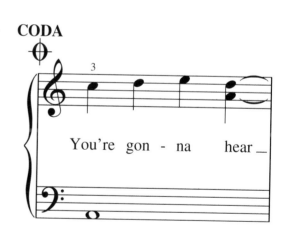

You're gon - na hear _

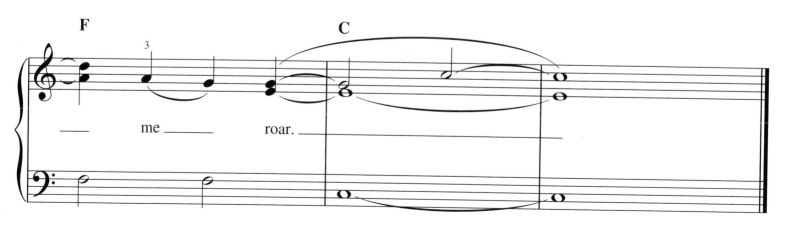

_ me _____ roar. _____

# SAFE AND SOUND

Words and Music by RYAN TAKACS MERCHANT
and SEBOUH (SEBU) SIMONIAN

I could lift   you up.
I could fill   your cup.

I could   show you what you wan-na   see and
You know my   riv - er won't e - vap - o - rate, this

take you where you wan-na   be. ___
world we still ap - pre - ci - ate. ___

You could be   my luck.
You could be   my luck.

E - ven
E - ven

if the sky is fall-in' down, I
in a hur - ri-cane of frowns, I

know that we'll be safe and   sound. ___
know that we'll be safe and   sound. ___

We're safe and sound. _

2.

Safe     and     sound,     we're safe  and     sound. _   Safe     and

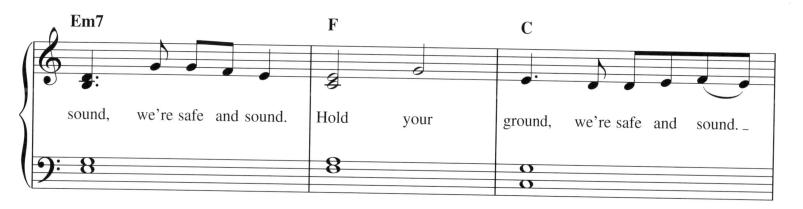

sound,     we're safe  and sound.   Hold     your     ground,   we're safe  and     sound. _

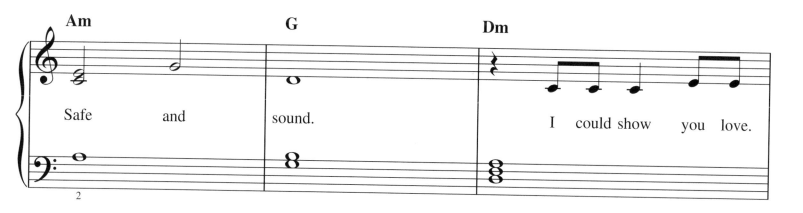

Safe     and     sound.     I  could show   you love.

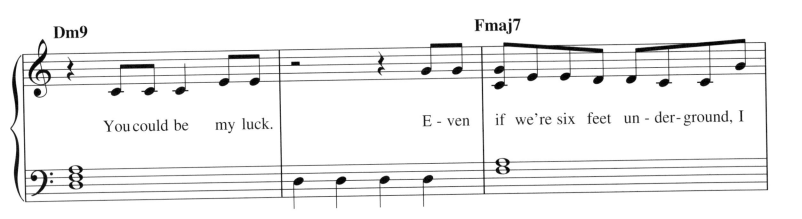

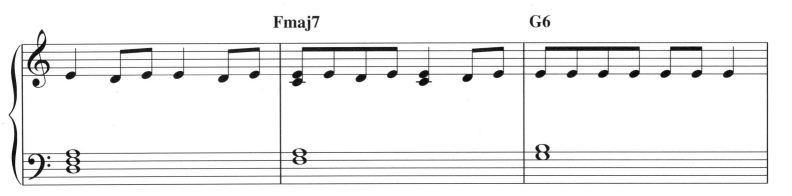

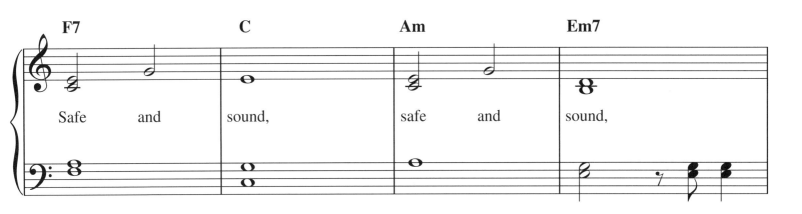

Safe and sound, safe and sound,

hold your ground, safe and sound.

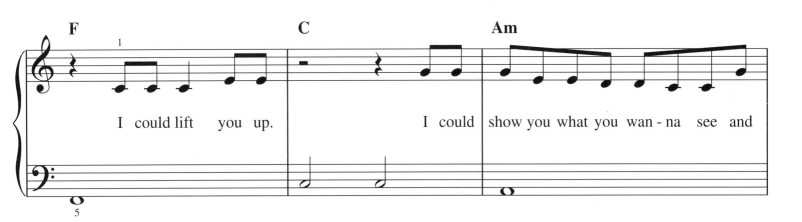

I could lift you up. I could show you what you wan-na see and

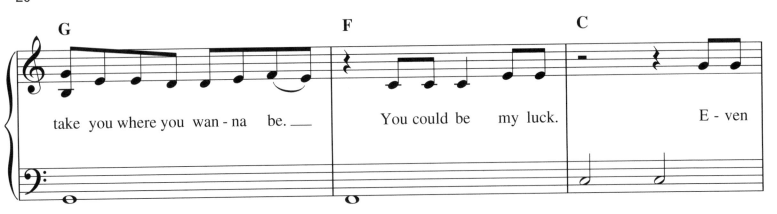

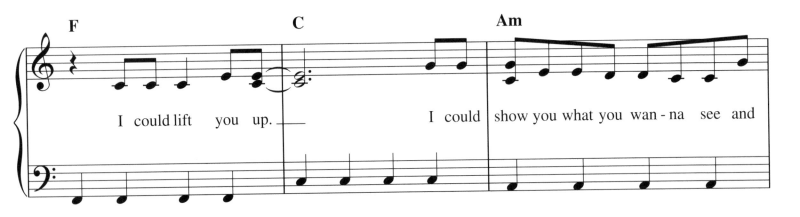

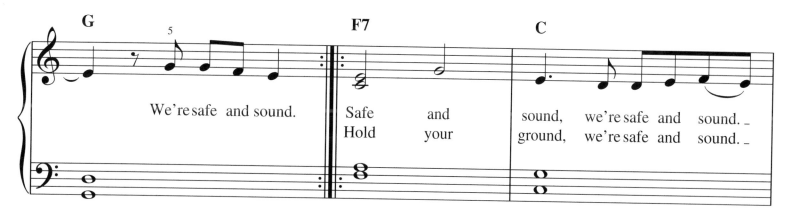

# WAKE ME UP!

Words and Music by TIM BERGLING,
ALOE BLACC and MICHAEL EINZIGER

jour - ney will end, but I know where to start. _____

They tell me I'm ___ too ___ young to un - der - stand.

They say I'm caught up in a dream. _ Well, life will pass me by if

I don't o - pen up my eyes. _____ Well, that's fine by me. _ So wake me

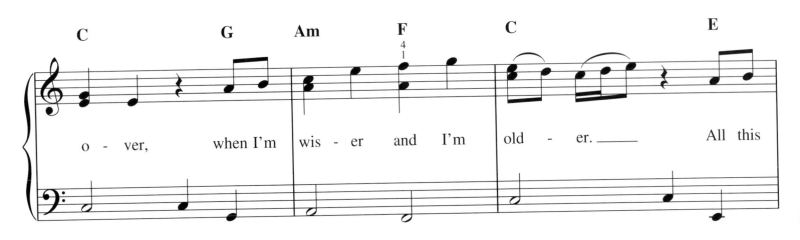

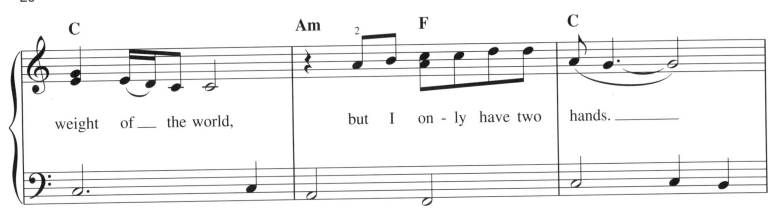

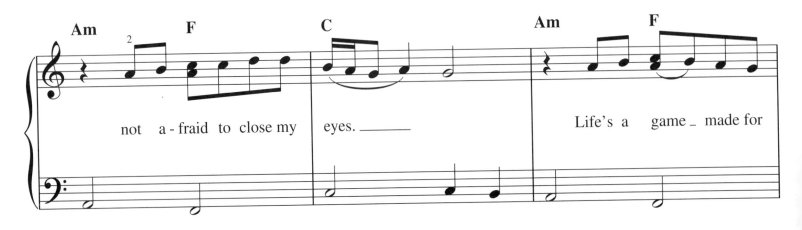

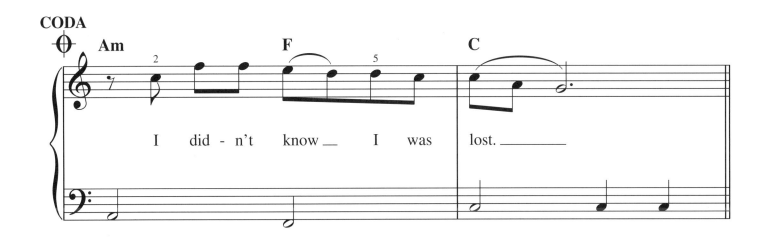

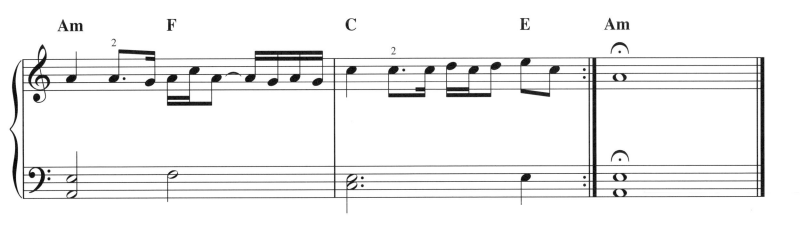

# ROYALS

Words and Music by JOEL LITTLE
and ELLA YELICH-O'CONNOR

**Moderately**

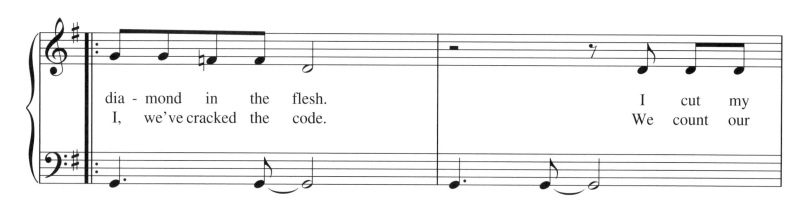

proud of my ad - dress. _____
one who knows us knows _____

In the torn - up
that we're fine with

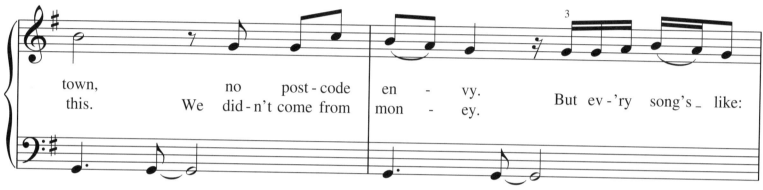

town,        no post - code    en - vy.
this.    We  did - n't come from  mon - ey.

But ev - 'ry song's _ like:

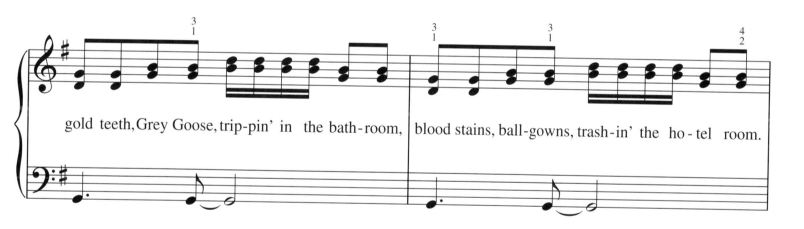

gold teeth, Grey Goose, trip - pin' in the bath - room,

blood stains, ball - gowns, trash - in' the ho - tel room.

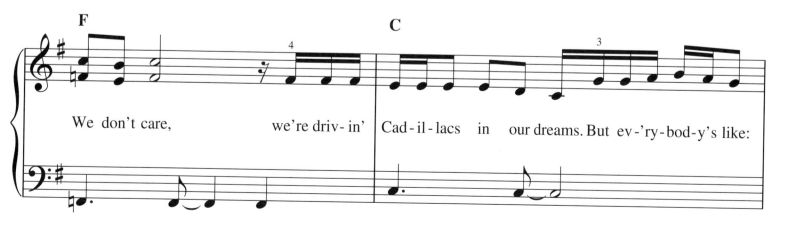

We don't care,        we're driv - in'

Cad - il - lacs in    our dreams. But ev - 'ry - bod - y's like:

To Coda ⊕

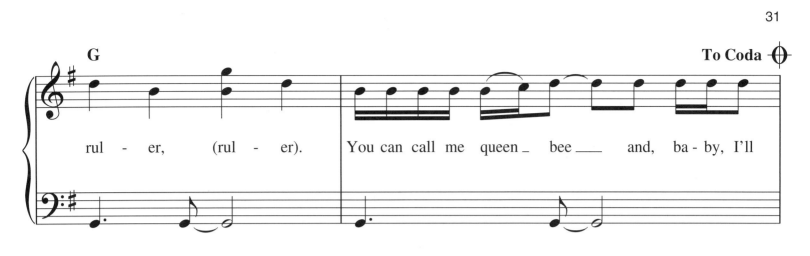

rul - er, (rul - er). You can call me queen_ bee __ and, ba - by, I'll

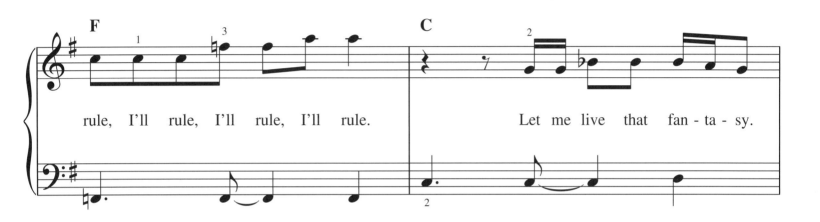

rule, I'll rule, I'll rule, I'll rule. Let me live that fan - ta - sy.

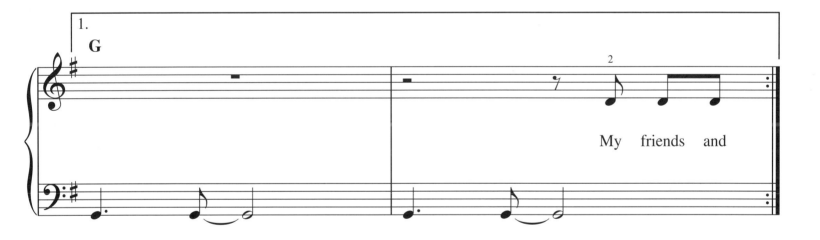

My friends and

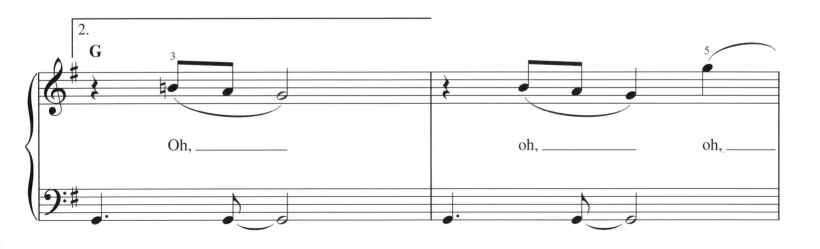

Oh, _____ oh, _____ oh, _____

we're big-ger than we ev - er dreamed. And I'm in love with be - ing queen. _

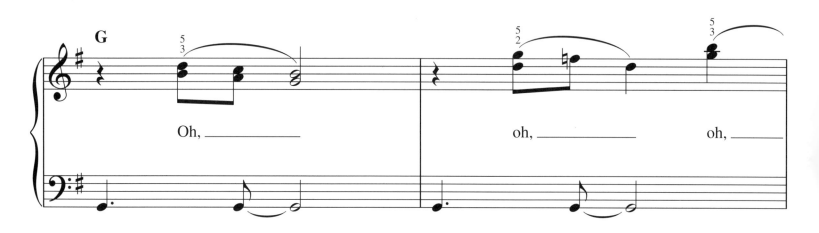

Oh, _____ oh, _____ oh, _____

D.S. al Coda

_ life is game with-out a care. We aren't caught up in your love af - fair. And we'll nev-er be

CODA

rule, I'll rule, I'll rule, I'll rule. Let me live that fan - ta - sy.